EMMANUEL JOSEPH

Speak, Lead, Act, Mastering Public Speaking, Leadership, and Relationships for Success

Copyright © 2025 by Emmanuel Joseph

All rights reserved. No part of this publication may be reproduced, stored or transmitted in any form or by any means, electronic, mechanical, photocopying, recording, scanning, or otherwise without written permission from the publisher. It is illegal to copy this book, post it to a website, or distribute it by any other means without permission.

First edition

This book was professionally typeset on Reedsy. Find out more at reedsy.com

Contents

1. Chapter 1: The Art of Communication — 1
2. Chapter 2: Overcoming Public Speaking Anxiety — 3
3. Chapter 3: Crafting Compelling Stories — 5
4. Chapter 4: Developing Leadership Qualities — 7
5. Chapter 5: Building Trust and Credibility — 9
6. Chapter 6: Active Listening and Empathy — 11
7. Chapter 7: Conflict Resolution Strategies — 13
8. Chapter 8: The Power of Nonverbal Communication — 15
9. Chapter 9: Building and Leading High-Performance Teams — 17
10. Chapter 10: The Role of Emotional Intelligence — 19
11. Chapter 11: Mastering Persuasion and Influence — 21
12. Chapter 12: Navigating Difficult Conversations — 23
13. Chapter 13: Cultivating a Growth Mindset — 25
14. Chapter 14: Effective Time Management — 27
15. Chapter 15: Building Resilience — 29
16. Chapter 16: Networking for Success — 31
17. Chapter 17: The Path to Continuous Improvement — 33

1

Chapter 1: The Art of Communication

Effective communication is the cornerstone of success in both personal and professional arenas. It involves more than just exchanging information; it's about understanding the emotions and intentions behind the words. Mastering the art of communication requires active listening, clarity, and empathy. As you embark on this journey, remember that great communicators are not born but made through consistent practice and dedication.

One of the key aspects of effective communication is active listening. This means fully concentrating on what is being said rather than just passively hearing the message of the speaker. Active listening involves giving full attention to the speaker, acknowledging their message, and responding thoughtfully. It's about being present in the moment and demonstrating genuine interest in the conversation. By practicing active listening, you can better understand the other person's perspective and respond in a meaningful way.

Clarity is another crucial component of effective communication. When you express your thoughts and ideas clearly, it reduces the chances of misunderstandings and ensures that your message is conveyed accurately. To achieve clarity, organize your thoughts before speaking, use simple and precise language, and avoid jargon or technical terms that the audience might not understand. Additionally, being concise and to the point helps to keep the listener engaged and focused on your message.

Empathy plays a vital role in communication as it allows you to connect with others on a deeper level. Empathy is the ability to understand and share the feelings of another person. By being empathetic, you can show that you genuinely care about the other person's emotions and experiences. This fosters trust and respect, making it easier to build strong relationships. To practice empathy, put yourself in the other person's shoes, listen without judgment, and validate their feelings.

Effective communication also involves nonverbal cues, such as body language, facial expressions, and tone of voice. These nonverbal signals can reinforce or contradict what is being said, so it's important to be mindful of them. For instance, maintaining eye contact can show confidence and sincerity, while slouching or crossing your arms might convey disinterest or defensiveness. By being aware of your nonverbal communication, you can ensure that your message is consistent and impactful.

2

Chapter 2: Overcoming Public Speaking Anxiety

Public speaking anxiety is a common fear that can hinder your ability to convey your message confidently. It's important to understand that feeling nervous is natural and can be managed with the right techniques. Practice deep breathing, visualization, and positive affirmations to calm your nerves. Remember, preparation and practice are key to building confidence and delivering an impactful speech.

One effective way to manage public speaking anxiety is through deep breathing exercises. When you feel nervous, your body responds by increasing your heart rate and breathing rate. By practicing deep breathing, you can slow down your heart rate and promote a sense of calm. Try taking slow, deep breaths in through your nose and out through your mouth. Focus on your breath and allow yourself to relax.

Visualization is another powerful technique to combat public speaking anxiety. Before your speech, take a few moments to visualize yourself delivering a successful presentation. Imagine the audience responding positively, and picture yourself speaking with confidence and clarity. Visualization helps to build a mental image of success, which can boost your confidence and reduce anxiety.

Positive affirmations can also help to alleviate public speaking anxiety.

Affirmations are positive statements that you repeat to yourself to build self-confidence and counter negative thoughts. For example, you might say to yourself, "I am a confident and engaging speaker," or "I am well-prepared and capable of delivering a great speech." By repeating these affirmations regularly, you can shift your mindset and reduce feelings of anxiety.

Preparation and practice are essential for building confidence in public speaking. The more prepared you are, the more confident you will feel. Start by thoroughly researching your topic and organizing your content into a clear and logical structure. Practice delivering your speech multiple times, and if possible, rehearse in front of a small audience or record yourself. Pay attention to your pacing, tone, and body language, and make adjustments as needed. The more you practice, the more comfortable you will become with your material, and the more confident you will feel on the day of your presentation.

3

Chapter 3: Crafting Compelling Stories

Storytelling is a powerful tool for engaging your audience and making your message memorable. A well-crafted story can illustrate your points, evoke emotions, and inspire action. To create compelling stories, focus on the structure: a captivating beginning, a meaningful middle, and a satisfying conclusion. Use vivid details and relatable characters to bring your story to life.

The beginning of your story should capture the audience's attention and draw them in. Start with a hook—something intriguing or surprising that piques their curiosity. This could be a provocative question, a startling fact, or an anecdote that sets the stage for your main message. The goal is to engage the audience right from the start and make them eager to hear more.

The middle of your story is where you develop the main events and build tension. This is the heart of your narrative, where you introduce the characters, describe the challenges they face, and illustrate their journey. Use vivid details to paint a picture in the audience's mind and make the story relatable. Focus on the emotions and experiences of the characters, as this helps to create an emotional connection with the audience.

The conclusion of your story should provide a satisfying resolution and reinforce your main message. It's important to tie up any loose ends and leave the audience with a clear takeaway. The conclusion should also evoke a sense of closure and completion, leaving the audience with a lasting impression.

Whether it's a lesson learned, an inspirational message, or a call to action, make sure your conclusion resonates with the audience and reinforces the purpose of your story.

In addition to structure, the elements of a compelling story include characters, conflict, and resolution. The characters should be relatable and believable, with distinct personalities and motivations. The conflict is the central challenge or problem that the characters face, and it drives the narrative forward. The resolution is how the characters overcome the conflict and achieve their goals. By incorporating these elements, you can create stories that captivate your audience and make your message memorable.

4

Chapter 4: Developing Leadership Qualities

Leadership is not just about holding a position of authority; it's about inspiring and guiding others towards a common goal. Key leadership qualities include integrity, vision, resilience, and empathy. By cultivating these traits, you can motivate and empower your team to achieve success. Remember, great leaders lead by example and are always willing to learn and grow.

Integrity is the foundation of effective leadership. It involves being honest, ethical, and consistent in your actions. Leaders with integrity build trust and credibility with their team members, as they demonstrate reliability and a strong moral compass. To cultivate integrity, always be truthful, honor your commitments, and act in alignment with your values.

Vision is another essential quality of a great leader. A clear and compelling vision provides direction and purpose for the team. It inspires and motivates team members to work towards a common goal. To develop your vision, identify your long-term objectives and articulate a clear plan for achieving them. Communicate your vision with passion and enthusiasm, and ensure that everyone understands their role in making it a reality.

Resilience is the ability to bounce back from setbacks and persist in the face of challenges. It's a crucial quality for leaders, as it enables them to navigate difficult situations and maintain a positive outlook. To build resilience, develop a growth mindset, practice self-care, and seek support from others. Embrace challenges as opportunities for growth and learn from your experiences.

Empathy is the ability to understand and share the feelings of others. It's an important quality for leaders, as it helps to build strong relationships and foster a supportive team environment. By being empathetic, you can show genuine concern for your team members' well-being and create a culture of trust and respect. Practice active listening, validate others' feelings, and offer support when needed.

Effective leadership also involves leading by example. Great leaders model the behavior they expect from their team members. They demonstrate a strong work ethic, maintain a positive attitude, and take responsibility for their actions. By setting a positive example, you can inspire and motivate your team to perform at their best.

5

Chapter 5: Building Trust and Credibility

Trust and credibility are the foundations of effective leadership and relationships. To build trust, be honest, transparent, and consistent in your actions. Show genuine concern for others and follow through on your commitments. Credibility comes from your expertise, experience, and the value you bring to your interactions. Earn trust by being reliable and demonstrating integrity.

To establish trust, always act with honesty and transparency. Being truthful and open with others fosters a sense of security and reliability. When you are transparent about your intentions, decisions, and actions, people are more likely to trust you. Additionally, admitting mistakes and taking responsibility for them shows integrity and builds credibility.

Consistency is another key factor in building trust. Consistent behavior and communication create predictability, which helps people feel secure in their interactions with you. When others know what to expect from you, they are more likely to trust your intentions and follow your lead. Be consistent in your actions, words, and values to maintain trust over time.

Showing genuine concern for others is essential for building strong relationships. Demonstrate empathy, listen actively, and offer support when needed. When people feel valued and understood, they are more likely to trust you and reciprocate with loyalty and commitment. Building trust requires ongoing effort and genuine care for the well-being of others.

Credibility is earned through your expertise, experience, and the value you bring to your interactions. Continuously develop your skills and knowledge to stay relevant and competent in your field. Share your expertise generously and provide valuable insights and solutions. When others see the positive impact of your contributions, your credibility will naturally grow.

6

Chapter 6: Active Listening and Empathy

A ctive listening and empathy are essential skills for building strong relationships and understanding others. Active listening involves fully engaging with the speaker, reflecting on their words, and responding thoughtfully. Empathy is the ability to understand and share the feelings of others. By practicing these skills, you can create a supportive environment and foster meaningful connections.

Active listening requires you to be fully present in the conversation. This means putting aside distractions, making eye contact, and focusing on the speaker. Show that you are listening by nodding, making verbal acknowledgments, and providing feedback. Reflect on the speaker's words by paraphrasing their message and asking clarifying questions. This demonstrates that you value their perspective and are actively engaged in the conversation.

Empathy involves understanding and sharing the feelings of others. It requires you to put yourself in the other person's shoes and see the situation from their perspective. Show empathy by validating their emotions and expressing genuine concern for their well-being. Avoid judgment and offer support in a compassionate and non-judgmental manner. By practicing empathy, you can build trust and create a safe space for open communication.

Active listening and empathy go hand in hand. When you actively listen to others, you gain a deeper understanding of their emotions and experiences.

This allows you to respond with empathy and provide meaningful support. By fostering these skills, you can strengthen your relationships and create a positive and inclusive environment.

7

Chapter 7: Conflict Resolution Strategies

Conflict is inevitable in any relationship, but it doesn't have to be destructive. Effective conflict resolution involves addressing issues constructively and finding mutually beneficial solutions. Key strategies include staying calm, actively listening, and seeking to understand the other person's perspective. Approach conflicts with an open mind and a willingness to compromise.

The first step in conflict resolution is to stay calm and composed. When emotions run high, it can be challenging to think clearly and communicate effectively. Take a few deep breaths and approach the situation with a calm and rational mindset. This helps to de-escalate tension and create a conducive environment for resolving the conflict.

Active listening is crucial in conflict resolution. Listen to the other person's concerns without interrupting or becoming defensive. Show that you understand their perspective by reflecting on their words and asking clarifying questions. This demonstrates that you value their viewpoint and are willing to work towards a resolution.

Seek to understand the root cause of the conflict. Often, conflicts arise from misunderstandings or unmet needs. By identifying the underlying issues, you can address them effectively and find a resolution that satisfies both parties. Focus on the problem, not the person, and avoid blaming or criticizing.

Approach conflicts with an open mind and a willingness to compromise.

Be flexible and explore different solutions that meet the needs of both parties. Look for win-win outcomes that benefit everyone involved. By working collaboratively and finding common ground, you can resolve conflicts constructively and maintain positive relationships.

8

Chapter 8: The Power of Nonverbal Communication

Nonverbal communication, such as body language, facial expressions, and tone of voice, plays a significant role in conveying your message. It can reinforce or contradict your words, so it's essential to be aware of your nonverbal cues. Practice maintaining eye contact, using appropriate gestures, and adopting a confident posture. By mastering nonverbal communication, you can enhance your overall effectiveness as a speaker and leader.

Body language is a powerful form of nonverbal communication. It includes gestures, posture, and movements that convey your emotions and intentions. Maintaining an open and confident posture, such as standing tall and uncrossing your arms, can signal confidence and approachability. Use gestures to emphasize key points and engage your audience.

Facial expressions are another important aspect of nonverbal communication. They convey emotions and can enhance or detract from your message. Smile to show friendliness, raise your eyebrows to express surprise, or frown to indicate concern. Be mindful of your facial expressions and ensure they align with your words.

Tone of voice also plays a crucial role in communication. It includes the pitch, volume, and speed of your speech. A warm and friendly tone can create a positive and inviting atmosphere, while a monotone or harsh tone can create distance and disinterest. Vary your tone to keep the audience engaged and convey the appropriate emotions.

Eye contact is a powerful way to connect with your audience. It shows confidence, sincerity, and attentiveness. Maintaining eye contact helps to build trust and credibility, as it demonstrates that you are fully engaged in the conversation. Be mindful of cultural differences, as the interpretation of eye contact can vary across cultures.

By mastering nonverbal communication, you can enhance your overall effectiveness as a communicator. Be aware of your body language, facial expressions, tone of voice, and eye contact. Ensure that your nonverbal cues align with your words to reinforce your message and create a positive impression.

9

Chapter 9: Building and Leading High-Performance Teams

Creating a high-performance team requires a clear vision, strong leadership, and effective communication. As a leader, your role is to inspire, motivate, and support your team members. Foster a positive and inclusive culture, encourage collaboration, and provide opportunities for growth and development. By building a cohesive and motivated team, you can achieve outstanding results.

To build a high-performance team, start by establishing a clear and compelling vision. This vision should outline the team's goals and objectives and provide a sense of direction and purpose. Communicate this vision with enthusiasm and ensure that every team member understands their role in achieving it. A shared vision creates alignment and motivates the team to work towards common goals.

Strong leadership is essential for guiding and supporting your team. Lead by example and demonstrate the values and behaviors you expect from your team members. Provide clear expectations and offer regular feedback and recognition. Empower your team by delegating responsibilities and trusting them to make decisions. Support their growth and development by providing opportunities for learning and advancement.

Effective communication is key to fostering collaboration and ensuring that everyone is on the same page. Encourage open and transparent communication within the team. Create an environment where team members feel comfortable sharing their ideas, concerns, and feedback. Hold regular team meetings to discuss progress, address challenges, and celebrate successes. Effective communication builds trust and strengthens team cohesion.

Fostering a positive and inclusive culture is crucial for building a high-performance team. Create an environment where diversity is valued, and everyone feels respected and included. Encourage collaboration and teamwork by promoting a culture of mutual support and respect. Recognize and celebrate the unique strengths and contributions of each team member. A positive and inclusive culture enhances team morale and boosts overall performance.

10

Chapter 10: The Role of Emotional Intelligence

Emotional intelligence (EI) is the ability to recognize, understand, and manage your emotions and the emotions of others. High EI is crucial for effective leadership and relationship-building. Develop your EI by practicing self-awareness, self-regulation, empathy, and social skills. By enhancing your emotional intelligence, you can navigate complex social dynamics and build stronger connections.

Self-awareness is the foundation of emotional intelligence. It involves recognizing and understanding your emotions and their impact on your thoughts and behaviors. Practice self-reflection and mindfulness to increase your self-awareness. Pay attention to your emotional responses and identify patterns in your behavior. By understanding your emotions, you can manage them more effectively.

Self-regulation is the ability to manage your emotions and behaviors in a healthy and constructive way. It involves staying calm and composed in stressful situations, controlling impulsive behaviors, and adapting to changing circumstances. Practice techniques such as deep breathing, meditation, and positive self-talk to enhance your self-regulation skills. By managing your emotions, you can respond to challenges with resilience and clarity.

Empathy is the ability to understand and share the feelings of others. It involves putting yourself in someone else's shoes and seeing the situation from their perspective. Practice active listening and seek to understand the emotions and experiences of others. Show genuine concern and offer support when needed. By practicing empathy, you can build trust and create meaningful connections.

Social skills are essential for building and maintaining positive relationships. They include effective communication, conflict resolution, and collaboration. Practice active listening, assertive communication, and constructive feedback to enhance your social skills. Build rapport and establish trust with others by being authentic and respectful. By developing strong social skills, you can navigate social interactions with confidence and ease.

11

Chapter 11: Mastering Persuasion and Influence

Persuasion and influence are essential skills for achieving your goals and inspiring others to take action. To be persuasive, understand your audience's needs, values, and motivations. Use logical arguments, emotional appeals, and credible evidence to make your case. Remember, ethical persuasion respects the autonomy of others and seeks to create win-win outcomes.

Understanding your audience is the first step in effective persuasion. Identify their needs, values, and motivations, and tailor your message accordingly. Consider what matters most to them and how your proposal aligns with their interests. By addressing their concerns and highlighting the benefits, you can make a compelling case for your perspective.

Logical arguments are an important aspect of persuasion. Use clear and rational reasoning to support your points. Provide evidence, data, and examples to back up your claims. Ensure that your arguments are well-structured and logically sound. A strong logical foundation enhances the credibility of your message.

Emotional appeals can also be powerful in persuasion. People are often influenced by their emotions, so tap into their feelings to create a connection. Use stories, anecdotes, and vivid imagery to evoke emotions and make your message memorable. Appeal to their values, aspirations, and fears to resonate on a deeper level. However, be careful not to manipulate emotions in a way that undermines trust.

Credibility is crucial for effective persuasion. Build credibility by demonstrating your expertise, experience, and integrity. Use credible sources and references to support your arguments. Show that you have done your research and are knowledgeable about the topic. When people trust your credibility, they are more likely to be persuaded by your message.

12

Chapter 12: Navigating Difficult Conversations

Difficult conversations are inevitable, but they can be handled with grace and effectiveness. Prepare by clarifying your goals, anticipating potential challenges, and planning your approach. During the conversation, stay calm, listen actively, and express your thoughts and feelings clearly. Seek to understand the other person's perspective and work towards a constructive resolution.

Preparation is key to navigating difficult conversations. Clarify your goals and objectives before entering the conversation. What do you hope to achieve, and what outcomes are acceptable to you? Anticipate potential challenges and think about how you will address them. Plan your approach and consider the best timing and setting for the conversation.

During the conversation, it's important to stay calm and composed. Take deep breaths and manage your emotions to ensure that you can think clearly and communicate effectively. Stay focused on the issue at hand and avoid getting sidetracked by emotional reactions. Maintaining a calm demeanor helps to create a conducive environment for resolving the conflict.

Active listening is crucial in difficult conversations. Listen to the other person's concerns without interrupting or becoming defensive. Show that you understand their perspective by reflecting on their words and asking clarifying questions. This demonstrates that you value their viewpoint and are committed to finding a resolution.

Express your thoughts and feelings clearly and assertively. Use "I" statements to convey your perspective without blaming or criticizing the other person. For example, say "I feel concerned when…" instead of "You always…" This helps to communicate your emotions and needs in a constructive way.

Seek to understand the other person's perspective and find common ground. Look for mutually beneficial solutions and be willing to compromise. Approach the conversation with an open mind and a willingness to collaborate. By working together, you can find a resolution that satisfies both parties and strengthens the relationship.

13

Chapter 13: Cultivating a Growth Mindset

A growth mindset is the belief that abilities and intelligence can be developed through effort and learning. Embrace challenges, persist in the face of setbacks, and view feedback as an opportunity for growth. Encourage a growth mindset in yourself and others by celebrating effort and progress. By cultivating a growth mindset, you can achieve continuous improvement and success.

Embracing challenges is a key aspect of a growth mindset. Instead of avoiding difficult tasks, see them as opportunities to learn and grow. Approach challenges with curiosity and a positive attitude. Recognize that setbacks and failures are part of the learning process and use them as stepping stones to improve your skills and knowledge.

Persistence is crucial when facing obstacles. A growth mindset involves maintaining determination and resilience, even when things get tough. Keep pushing forward and stay focused on your goals. Remember that progress may be slow, but every step forward is a step closer to success. Celebrate small victories and acknowledge the effort you put into overcoming challenges.

Feedback is an invaluable tool for growth. Instead of viewing feedback as criticism, see it as constructive guidance to help you improve. Actively seek feedback from others and use it to refine your skills and strategies.

Reflect on the feedback and identify areas where you can make adjustments. By embracing feedback, you can continuously develop and enhance your abilities.

Encourage a growth mindset in others by recognizing and celebrating their efforts and progress. Provide positive reinforcement and support their learning journey. Create an environment where mistakes are seen as learning opportunities, and everyone is encouraged to take risks and innovate. By fostering a growth mindset culture, you can inspire continuous improvement and drive collective success.

14

Chapter 14: Effective Time Management

Time management is crucial for achieving your goals and maintaining a healthy work-life balance. Prioritize tasks based on their importance and urgency, and create a structured schedule to stay on track. Use techniques such as the Pomodoro Technique and time blocking to enhance your productivity. Remember, effective time management involves setting boundaries and avoiding burnout.

Prioritizing tasks is the first step in effective time management. Identify the most important and urgent tasks and focus on completing them first. Use tools like the Eisenhower Matrix to categorize tasks based on their importance and urgency. This helps you allocate your time and energy to the tasks that matter most and avoid getting overwhelmed by less critical activities.

Creating a structured schedule is essential for staying organized and on track. Plan your day or week in advance, allocating specific time slots for each task. Use digital calendars, planners, or time management apps to keep track of your schedule. Be realistic about the time required for each task and build in buffer time for unexpected interruptions or delays.

The Pomodoro Technique is a popular time management method that involves working in focused intervals, usually 25 minutes, followed by a short break. This helps to maintain concentration and prevent burnout. Set a timer for 25 minutes and work on a specific task without distractions. After the timer goes off, take a 5-minute break before starting the next interval. Repeat this process and take a longer break after completing four intervals.

Time blocking is another effective technique for managing your time. This involves allocating specific blocks of time for different activities or tasks. For example, you might designate the morning for focused work, the afternoon for meetings, and the evening for personal time. By creating dedicated time blocks, you can minimize distractions and ensure that you allocate sufficient time for each activity.

Setting boundaries is crucial for maintaining a healthy work-life balance. Define clear limits for your work hours and personal time. Communicate these boundaries to others and stick to them. Avoid overcommitting and learn to say no when necessary. Prioritize self-care and make time for activities that recharge and rejuvenate you. By setting boundaries, you can prevent burnout and maintain your overall well-being.

15

Chapter 15: Building Resilience

Resilience is the ability to bounce back from adversity and thrive in the face of challenges. Develop resilience by cultivating a positive outlook, practicing self-care, and building a strong support network. Learn from setbacks and view them as opportunities for growth. By building resilience, you can navigate life's ups and downs with grace and determination.

Cultivating a positive outlook is essential for building resilience. Focus on the positives in any situation and maintain an optimistic mindset. Practice gratitude by regularly acknowledging the things you are thankful for. Reframe challenges as opportunities for growth and learning. By maintaining a positive outlook, you can build the mental and emotional strength needed to overcome adversity.

Self-care is crucial for maintaining resilience. Take care of your physical, emotional, and mental well-being. Prioritize regular exercise, a healthy diet, and sufficient sleep. Engage in activities that bring you joy and relaxation, such as hobbies, meditation, or spending time in nature. By taking care of yourself, you can build the resilience needed to handle stress and challenges effectively.

Building a strong support network is another important aspect of resilience. Surround yourself with positive and supportive people who uplift and encourage you. Seek out mentors, friends, and colleagues who can provide guidance and support during difficult times. Don't be afraid to ask for help when needed. A strong support network can provide emotional support, practical advice, and a sense of belonging.

Learning from setbacks is key to developing resilience. View failures and challenges as opportunities for growth and improvement. Reflect on your experiences and identify lessons learned. Use setbacks as a chance to develop new skills and strategies. By adopting a growth mindset and learning from your experiences, you can build the resilience needed to navigate future challenges.

16

Chapter 16: Networking for Success

Networking is a valuable skill for building relationships and creating opportunities. Approach networking with a genuine interest in others and a willingness to offer help. Attend events, join professional organizations, and leverage social media to expand your network. Build meaningful connections by staying in touch and providing value to your contacts.

Approach networking with a mindset of giving rather than taking. Focus on building genuine relationships and offering help to others. Show a genuine interest in people's backgrounds, experiences, and goals. Ask questions and listen actively to understand their needs and aspirations. By demonstrating a willingness to help, you can build trust and create mutually beneficial connections.

Attending events and joining professional organizations are great ways to expand your network. Participate in industry conferences, seminars, and networking events to meet new people and exchange ideas. Join professional associations or groups related to your field to connect with like-minded individuals. Take advantage of opportunities to collaborate and share knowledge with others.

Leverage social media platforms to expand your network and stay connected with contacts. Use LinkedIn to connect with professionals in your industry and engage with their content. Share valuable insights, articles, and updates to showcase your expertise. Participate in online discussions and join relevant groups to expand your reach. Social media provides a convenient way to maintain and grow your network.

Building meaningful connections involves staying in touch and providing value to your contacts. Follow up after meeting someone new and express your appreciation for the connection. Stay engaged by checking in periodically and offering support when needed. Share valuable resources, insights, or opportunities that may benefit your contacts. By nurturing your relationships, you can build a strong and supportive network.

17

Chapter 17: The Path to Continuous Improvement

Success is a journey, not a destination. Commit to lifelong learning and continuous improvement in all areas of your life. Seek feedback, embrace new challenges, and stay curious. Reflect on your experiences and use them to grow and evolve. By pursuing continuous improvement, you can achieve your full potential and make a lasting impact.

Lifelong learning is the key to continuous improvement. Stay curious and open to new knowledge and experiences. Invest in your personal and professional development by seeking out learning opportunities, such as courses, workshops, and seminars. Stay updated on industry trends and advancements. Embrace a mindset of growth and development, and never stop seeking ways to improve.

Feedback is a valuable tool for growth. Actively seek feedback from others and use it to refine your skills and strategies. Be open to constructive criticism and view it as an opportunity for improvement. Reflect on the feedback and identify areas where you can make adjustments. By incorporating feedback into your development, you can achieve continuous improvement.

Embrace new challenges and step out of your comfort zone. Take on tasks and projects that push your boundaries and require you to develop new skills. View challenges as opportunities to learn and grow. By embracing new experiences, you can expand your capabilities and achieve greater success.

Reflection is an important practice for continuous improvement. Regularly take time to reflect on your experiences, successes, and setbacks. Identify lessons learned and areas for growth. Use reflection to set new goals and create a plan for achieving them. By reflecting on your journey, you can stay focused on continuous improvement and make meaningful progress.

Speak, Lead, Act: Mastering Public Speaking, Leadership, and Relationships for Success

In an ever-evolving world, mastering the art of communication, leadership, and relationship-building is essential for achieving success. "Speak, Lead, Act" is your comprehensive guide to developing these crucial skills and transforming your personal and professional life.

This book takes you on a journey through the fundamentals of effective communication, from overcoming public speaking anxiety to crafting compelling stories that captivate your audience. Discover the power of nonverbal communication, active listening, and empathy as you build trust and credibility in your interactions.

Learn to develop key leadership qualities such as integrity, vision, resilience, and emotional intelligence. Explore practical strategies for building and leading high-performance teams, navigating difficult conversations, and resolving conflicts constructively. With insights on persuasion, influence, and networking, you'll gain the tools to inspire others and create meaningful connections.

"Speak, Lead, Act" also emphasizes the importance of a growth mindset, effective time management, and resilience in achieving continuous improvement and success. Whether you're a seasoned professional or just starting your journey, this book provides valuable guidance and actionable tips to help you thrive in every aspect of your life.

Empower yourself with the knowledge and skills to communicate confidently, lead with purpose, and build strong relationships. "Speak, Lead, Act" is your roadmap to success in today's dynamic world.

www.ingramcontent.com/pod-product-compliance
Lightning Source LLC
LaVergne TN
LVHW020458080526
838202LV00057B/6021